50 Creative International Pizza Dishes

By: Kelly Johnson

Table of Contents

- Mexican Taco Pizza
- Japanese Teriyaki Chicken Pizza
- Indian Butter Chicken Pizza
- Greek Gyro Pizza
- Thai Peanut Chicken Pizza
- Korean Bulgogi Beef Pizza
- French Ratatouille Pizza
- Middle Eastern Shawarma Pizza
- Caribbean Jerk Chicken Pizza
- Argentinian Chimichurri Steak Pizza
- Hawaiian BBQ Pizza
- Spanish Chorizo and Manchego Pizza
- Italian Caprese Pizza
- German Sauerkraut and Sausage Pizza
- Russian Beef Stroganoff Pizza
- Chinese Sweet and Sour Pork Pizza
- Brazilian Feijoada Pizza
- Moroccan Spiced Lamb Pizza
- Swedish Meatball Pizza
- Lebanese Za'atar Flatbread Pizza
- Australian Vegemite and Cheese Pizza
- Polish Kielbasa and Cabbage Pizza
- Vietnamese Banh Mi Pizza
- Ethiopian Berbere Spiced Pizza
- Peruvian Aji de Gallina Pizza
- Canadian Poutine Pizza
- South African Bobotie Pizza
- Filipino Adobo Chicken Pizza
- Turkish Lahmacun Pizza
- Italian Quattro Formaggi Pizza
- Argentinean Provoleta Pizza
- Greek Spanakopita Pizza
- Korean Kimchi and Pork Belly Pizza
- Indian Paneer Tikka Pizza
- Malaysian Satay Pizza

- Jamaican Ackee and Saltfish Pizza
- Thai Green Curry Pizza
- Moroccan Harissa Chicken Pizza
- Brazilian BBQ (Churrasco) Pizza
- Swiss Fondue Cheese Pizza
- Hungarian Goulash Pizza
- Egyptian Fava Bean (Ful Medames) Pizza
- Pakistani Seekh Kebab Pizza
- Indonesian Rendang Beef Pizza
- French Croque Monsieur Pizza
- Chinese Peking Duck Pizza
- Italian Prosciutto and Fig Pizza
- Puerto Rican Mofongo Pizza
- Scandinavian Smoked Salmon Pizza
- Indian Samosa-Inspired Pizza

Mexican Taco Pizza

Ingredients:

- 1 pre-made pizza crust
- 1/2 cup refried beans
- 1/2 cup salsa
- 1 cup shredded cheddar cheese
- 1 cup cooked taco-seasoned ground beef
- 1/2 cup diced tomatoes
- 1/2 cup shredded lettuce
- 1/4 cup sliced black olives
- Sour cream and guacamole for topping

Instructions:

1. Preheat oven to 400°F (200°C).
2. Spread refried beans over the pizza crust, followed by salsa.
3. Sprinkle with cheese and add taco-seasoned ground beef.
4. Bake for 10-12 minutes or until cheese is melted and bubbly.
5. Top with lettuce, tomatoes, and olives. Serve with sour cream and guacamole.

Japanese Teriyaki Chicken Pizza

Ingredients:

- 1 pre-made pizza crust
- 1/4 cup teriyaki sauce
- 1 cup shredded mozzarella cheese
- 1 cup cooked teriyaki chicken, sliced
- 1/2 cup thinly sliced red onions
- 1/4 cup chopped green onions
- 1 tbsp sesame seeds

Instructions:

1. Preheat oven to 425°F (220°C).
2. Spread teriyaki sauce over the pizza crust.
3. Add mozzarella cheese, chicken, and red onions.
4. Bake for 10-15 minutes or until cheese is melted and golden.
5. Garnish with green onions and sesame seeds before serving.

Indian Butter Chicken Pizza

Ingredients:

- 1 naan bread or pizza crust
- 1/2 cup butter chicken sauce
- 1 cup cooked butter chicken
- 1 cup shredded mozzarella cheese
- 1/4 cup thinly sliced red onions
- Fresh cilantro for garnish

Instructions:

1. Preheat oven to 400°F (200°C).
2. Spread butter chicken sauce over the naan or crust.
3. Add cooked butter chicken, mozzarella, and red onions.
4. Bake for 8-10 minutes or until cheese is melted.
5. Garnish with fresh cilantro before serving.

Greek Gyro Pizza

Ingredients:

- 1 pita bread or pizza crust
- 1/2 cup tzatziki sauce
- 1 cup cooked gyro meat slices
- 1/2 cup chopped tomatoes
- 1/4 cup sliced red onions
- 1/4 cup crumbled feta cheese
- 1 tbsp chopped fresh dill

Instructions:

1. Preheat oven to 400°F (200°C).
2. Spread tzatziki sauce over the crust.
3. Layer with gyro meat, tomatoes, red onions, and feta cheese.
4. Bake for 8-10 minutes.
5. Garnish with fresh dill before serving.

Thai Peanut Chicken Pizza

Ingredients:

- 1 pre-made pizza crust
- 1/4 cup peanut sauce
- 1 cup shredded mozzarella cheese
- 1 cup cooked chicken, shredded
- 1/2 cup shredded carrots
- 1/4 cup chopped peanuts
- 1 tbsp chopped fresh cilantro

Instructions:

1. Preheat oven to 425°F (220°C).
2. Spread peanut sauce over the crust and sprinkle with mozzarella cheese.
3. Top with chicken and carrots.
4. Bake for 10-12 minutes.
5. Garnish with peanuts and cilantro before serving.

Korean Bulgogi Beef Pizza

Ingredients:

- 1 pizza crust
- 1/4 cup gochujang sauce (Korean chili paste, diluted with a bit of water)
- 1 cup cooked bulgogi beef (marinated in soy sauce, sugar, garlic, and sesame oil)
- 1 cup shredded mozzarella cheese
- 1/4 cup sliced green onions
- 1 tsp sesame seeds

Instructions:

1. Preheat oven to 425°F (220°C).
2. Spread gochujang sauce over the crust.
3. Add mozzarella cheese and top with bulgogi beef.
4. Bake for 10-12 minutes.
5. Garnish with green onions and sesame seeds.

French Ratatouille Pizza

Ingredients:

- 1 pizza crust
- 1/2 cup tomato sauce
- 1/2 cup thinly sliced zucchini
- 1/2 cup thinly sliced eggplant
- 1/2 cup thinly sliced bell peppers
- 1/4 cup sliced black olives
- 1/2 cup shredded mozzarella cheese
- Fresh basil leaves for garnish

Instructions:

1. Preheat oven to 400°F (200°C).
2. Spread tomato sauce over the crust.
3. Arrange zucchini, eggplant, bell peppers, and olives.
4. Sprinkle with mozzarella cheese.
5. Bake for 12-15 minutes and garnish with basil leaves.

Middle Eastern Shawarma Pizza

Ingredients:

- 1 pita bread or pizza crust
- 1/2 cup hummus
- 1 cup cooked chicken shawarma slices
- 1/4 cup sliced red onions
- 1/4 cup chopped cucumbers
- 1/4 cup diced tomatoes
- 1 tbsp chopped parsley

Instructions:

1. Preheat oven to 400°F (200°C).
2. Spread hummus over the crust.
3. Add shawarma slices, red onions, cucumbers, and tomatoes.
4. Bake for 8-10 minutes.
5. Garnish with parsley before serving.

Caribbean Jerk Chicken Pizza

Ingredients:

- 1 pizza crust
- 1/4 cup jerk marinade
- 1 cup cooked jerk chicken, shredded
- 1 cup shredded mozzarella cheese
- 1/4 cup chopped pineapple
- 1/4 cup sliced red bell peppers
- Fresh cilantro for garnish

Instructions:

1. Preheat oven to 425°F (220°C).
2. Spread jerk marinade over the crust.
3. Add mozzarella cheese, chicken, pineapple, and bell peppers.
4. Bake for 10-12 minutes.
5. Garnish with fresh cilantro before serving.

Argentinian Chimichurri Steak Pizza

Ingredients:

- 1 pizza crust
- 1/4 cup chimichurri sauce (homemade or store-bought)
- 1 cup thinly sliced grilled steak
- 1 cup shredded mozzarella cheese
- 1/4 cup thinly sliced red onions
- Fresh parsley for garnish

Instructions:

1. Preheat oven to 425°F (220°C).
2. Spread chimichurri sauce over the pizza crust.
3. Add mozzarella cheese, steak slices, and red onions.
4. Bake for 10-12 minutes or until cheese is melted.
5. Garnish with fresh parsley before serving.

Hawaiian BBQ Pizza

Ingredients:

- 1 pizza crust
- 1/4 cup barbecue sauce
- 1 cup shredded mozzarella cheese
- 1/2 cup diced ham
- 1/2 cup pineapple chunks
- 1/4 cup sliced red onions

Instructions:

1. Preheat oven to 400°F (200°C).
2. Spread barbecue sauce over the crust.
3. Add mozzarella, ham, pineapple, and red onions.
4. Bake for 10-12 minutes.
5. Serve hot and enjoy!

Spanish Chorizo and Manchego Pizza

Ingredients:

- 1 pizza crust
- 1/2 cup tomato sauce
- 1/2 cup shredded Manchego cheese
- 1/2 cup sliced Spanish chorizo
- 1/4 cup roasted red peppers
- 1 tbsp chopped fresh parsley

Instructions:

1. Preheat oven to 425°F (220°C).
2. Spread tomato sauce over the crust.
3. Add Manchego cheese, chorizo, and roasted red peppers.
4. Bake for 10-12 minutes.
5. Garnish with parsley before serving.

Italian Caprese Pizza

Ingredients:

- 1 pizza crust
- 1/4 cup olive oil
- 1 cup fresh mozzarella slices
- 1 cup sliced tomatoes
- Fresh basil leaves
- Balsamic glaze for drizzling

Instructions:

1. Preheat oven to 400°F (200°C).
2. Brush the crust with olive oil.
3. Add mozzarella and tomato slices.
4. Bake for 8-10 minutes or until cheese is melted.
5. Top with basil leaves and drizzle with balsamic glaze.

German Sauerkraut and Sausage Pizza

Ingredients:

- 1 pizza crust
- 1/4 cup mustard-based sauce (or Dijon mustard mixed with a little honey)
- 1 cup shredded Swiss cheese
- 1/2 cup cooked bratwurst slices
- 1/2 cup sauerkraut, drained

Instructions:

1. Preheat oven to 400°F (200°C).
2. Spread mustard sauce over the crust.
3. Add Swiss cheese, bratwurst slices, and sauerkraut.
4. Bake for 10-12 minutes.
5. Serve warm and enjoy!

Russian Beef Stroganoff Pizza

Ingredients:

- 1 pizza crust
- 1/4 cup sour cream or cream sauce
- 1 cup cooked beef stroganoff (thinly sliced beef in creamy sauce)
- 1 cup shredded mozzarella cheese
- 1/4 cup sautéed mushrooms
- Fresh dill for garnish

Instructions:

1. Preheat oven to 425°F (220°C).
2. Spread sour cream or cream sauce over the crust.
3. Add mozzarella, beef, and mushrooms.
4. Bake for 10-12 minutes.
5. Garnish with fresh dill before serving.

Chinese Sweet and Sour Pork Pizza

Ingredients:

- 1 pizza crust
- 1/4 cup sweet and sour sauce
- 1 cup cooked pork (bite-sized pieces)
- 1/2 cup pineapple chunks
- 1/2 cup thinly sliced bell peppers
- 1/4 cup shredded mozzarella cheese

Instructions:

1. Preheat oven to 425°F (220°C).
2. Spread sweet and sour sauce over the crust.
3. Add pork, pineapple, bell peppers, and mozzarella.
4. Bake for 10-12 minutes.
5. Serve immediately and enjoy!

Brazilian Feijoada Pizza

Ingredients:

- 1 pizza crust
- 1/4 cup black bean puree (seasoned with garlic and spices)
- 1 cup shredded mozzarella cheese
- 1/2 cup diced cooked sausage (linguiça or chorizo)
- 1/4 cup diced cooked pork
- 1/4 cup sliced collard greens

Instructions:

1. Preheat oven to 400°F (200°C).
2. Spread black bean puree over the crust.
3. Add mozzarella, sausage, pork, and collard greens.
4. Bake for 10-12 minutes.
5. Serve hot and enjoy a taste of Brazil!

Moroccan Spiced Lamb Pizza

Ingredients:

- 1 pizza crust
- 1/4 cup harissa sauce
- 1 cup cooked ground lamb (seasoned with Moroccan spices like cumin, cinnamon, and coriander)
- 1/2 cup crumbled feta cheese
- 1/4 cup chopped fresh mint and cilantro
- 1/4 cup thinly sliced red onions

Instructions:

1. Preheat oven to 425°F (220°C).
2. Spread harissa sauce over the crust.
3. Add ground lamb, feta, and red onions.
4. Bake for 10-12 minutes.
5. Garnish with mint and cilantro before serving.

Swedish Meatball Pizza

Ingredients:

- 1 pizza crust
- 1/4 cup cream sauce or béchamel
- 1 cup cooked Swedish meatballs, sliced
- 1/2 cup shredded mozzarella cheese
- 1/4 cup lingonberry jam (optional)
- Chopped parsley for garnish

Instructions:

1. Preheat oven to 400°F (200°C).
2. Spread cream sauce over the crust.
3. Add mozzarella and meatball slices.
4. Bake for 10-12 minutes.
5. Drizzle with lingonberry jam and garnish with parsley before serving.

Lebanese Za'atar Flatbread Pizza

Ingredients:

- 1 flatbread or thin pizza crust
- 2 tbsp olive oil
- 2 tbsp za'atar seasoning
- 1/2 cup crumbled goat cheese
- 1/4 cup cherry tomatoes, halved
- 1/4 cup fresh arugula

Instructions:

1. Preheat oven to 400°F (200°C).
2. Brush flatbread with olive oil and sprinkle with za'atar.
3. Add goat cheese and cherry tomatoes.
4. Bake for 8-10 minutes.
5. Top with arugula before serving.

Australian Vegemite and Cheese Pizza

Ingredients:

- 1 pizza crust
- 1-2 tsp Vegemite (spread thinly)
- 1 cup shredded cheddar cheese
- 1/4 cup sautéed onions (optional)

Instructions:

1. Preheat oven to 400°F (200°C).
2. Spread Vegemite thinly over the crust.
3. Add cheddar cheese and onions if desired.
4. Bake for 8-10 minutes.
5. Serve hot for a savory treat.

Polish Kielbasa and Cabbage Pizza

Ingredients:

- 1 pizza crust
- 1/4 cup mustard cream sauce (mix Dijon mustard with cream)
- 1/2 cup thinly sliced cooked kielbasa
- 1/2 cup sautéed cabbage and onions
- 1 cup shredded Swiss cheese

Instructions:

1. Preheat oven to 425°F (220°C).
2. Spread mustard cream sauce over the crust.
3. Add kielbasa, cabbage, onions, and Swiss cheese.
4. Bake for 10-12 minutes.
5. Enjoy a hearty Polish-inspired slice!

Vietnamese Banh Mi Pizza

Ingredients:

- 1 pizza crust
- 1/4 cup hoisin sauce
- 1 cup shredded pork or chicken
- 1/4 cup pickled carrots and daikon
- 1/4 cup sliced cucumbers
- Fresh cilantro and sliced jalapeños for garnish

Instructions:

1. Preheat oven to 400°F (200°C).
2. Spread hoisin sauce over the crust.
3. Add pork or chicken.
4. Bake for 8-10 minutes.
5. Top with pickled vegetables, cucumbers, cilantro, and jalapeños before serving.

Ethiopian Berbere Spiced Pizza

Ingredients:

- 1 pizza crust
- 1/4 cup tomato-based sauce with 1 tsp berbere spice blend
- 1 cup shredded spiced chicken or beef
- 1/2 cup crumbled feta cheese
- 1/4 cup sautéed onions and bell peppers

Instructions:

1. Preheat oven to 425°F (220°C).
2. Spread spiced tomato sauce over the crust.
3. Add chicken or beef, feta, onions, and bell peppers.
4. Bake for 10-12 minutes.
5. Serve with a sprinkle of additional berbere if desired.

Peruvian Aji de Gallina Pizza

Ingredients:

- 1 pizza crust
- 1/4 cup aji amarillo sauce
- 1 cup shredded chicken in a creamy aji amarillo sauce
- 1/4 cup sliced hard-boiled eggs
- 1/4 cup sliced black olives
- 1/2 cup shredded mozzarella cheese

Instructions:

1. Preheat oven to 400°F (200°C).
2. Spread aji amarillo sauce over the crust.
3. Add chicken, eggs, olives, and mozzarella.
4. Bake for 10-12 minutes.
5. Enjoy a Peruvian twist on pizza night!

Canadian Poutine Pizza

Ingredients:

- 1 pizza crust
- 1/2 cup brown gravy
- 1 cup shredded mozzarella or cheese curds
- 1/2 cup cooked, crispy French fries
- Chopped fresh parsley for garnish

Instructions:

1. Preheat oven to 400°F (200°C).
2. Spread gravy over the crust.
3. Add cheese curds or mozzarella and French fries.
4. Bake for 10-12 minutes.
5. Garnish with parsley and serve this indulgent Canadian creation.

South African Bobotie Pizza

Ingredients:

- 1 pizza crust
- 1/4 cup curry-flavored tomato sauce
- 1 cup spiced ground beef or lamb (prepared with bobotie spices: curry powder, turmeric, and chutney)
- 1/4 cup caramelized onions
- 1/4 cup golden raisins
- 1/4 cup shredded mozzarella cheese
- Chopped fresh cilantro for garnish

Instructions:

1. Preheat oven to 425°F (220°C).
2. Spread curry tomato sauce over the crust.
3. Add spiced ground meat, onions, raisins, and mozzarella.
4. Bake for 10-12 minutes.
5. Garnish with cilantro before serving.

Filipino Adobo Chicken Pizza

Ingredients:

- 1 pizza crust
- 1/4 cup soy sauce and vinegar glaze (reduce soy sauce and vinegar with sugar)
- 1 cup shredded adobo chicken
- 1/4 cup thinly sliced red onions
- 1/4 cup shredded mozzarella cheese
- Sliced scallions for garnish

Instructions:

1. Preheat oven to 400°F (200°C).
2. Spread soy sauce and vinegar glaze over the crust.
3. Add adobo chicken, onions, and mozzarella.
4. Bake for 10-12 minutes.
5. Top with scallions before serving.

Turkish Lahmacun Pizza

Ingredients:

- 1 thin pizza crust or flatbread
- 1/2 cup spiced ground lamb or beef (mixed with tomato paste, paprika, cumin, and parsley)
- 1/4 cup diced tomatoes
- 1/4 cup chopped parsley
- Lemon wedges for serving

Instructions:

1. Preheat oven to 400°F (200°C).
2. Spread spiced meat mixture thinly over the crust.
3. Bake for 8-10 minutes until crisp.
4. Garnish with fresh parsley and serve with lemon wedges for a zesty kick.

Italian Quattro Formaggi Pizza

Ingredients:

- 1 pizza crust
- 1/4 cup tomato sauce (optional, for a red base)
- 1/4 cup shredded mozzarella
- 1/4 cup crumbled gorgonzola
- 1/4 cup grated parmesan
- 1/4 cup fontina cheese slices

Instructions:

1. Preheat oven to 425°F (220°C).
2. Spread tomato sauce (if using) on the crust.
3. Distribute all cheeses evenly over the crust.
4. Bake for 10-12 minutes until bubbly and golden.
5. Serve immediately for a cheesy delight!

Argentinean Provoleta Pizza

Ingredients:

- 1 pizza crust
- 1 cup shredded provolone cheese
- 1/4 cup grilled vegetables (zucchini, peppers, and eggplant)
- Fresh oregano leaves for garnish

Instructions:

1. Preheat oven to 400°F (200°C).
2. Spread provolone cheese evenly on the crust.
3. Top with grilled vegetables.
4. Bake for 8-10 minutes until the cheese is melted and bubbly.
5. Garnish with fresh oregano before serving.

Greek Spanakopita Pizza

Ingredients:

- 1 pizza crust
- 1/4 cup olive oil and garlic base
- 1/2 cup sautéed spinach and onions
- 1/4 cup crumbled feta cheese
- 1/4 cup shredded mozzarella cheese
- 1/4 cup chopped fresh dill

Instructions:

1. Preheat oven to 425°F (220°C).
2. Spread olive oil and garlic mixture over the crust.
3. Add spinach, onions, feta, and mozzarella.
4. Bake for 10-12 minutes.
5. Garnish with fresh dill before serving.

Korean Kimchi and Pork Belly Pizza

Ingredients:

- 1 pizza crust
- 1/4 cup gochujang sauce (Korean chili paste mixed with honey)
- 1 cup cooked, thinly sliced pork belly
- 1/4 cup chopped kimchi
- 1/2 cup shredded mozzarella cheese
- Sliced green onions and sesame seeds for garnish

Instructions:

1. Preheat oven to 400°F (200°C).
2. Spread gochujang sauce over the crust.
3. Add pork belly, kimchi, and mozzarella.
4. Bake for 10-12 minutes.
5. Garnish with green onions and sesame seeds before serving.

Indian Paneer Tikka Pizza

Ingredients:

- 1 pizza crust
- 1/4 cup tikka masala sauce
- 1 cup cubed paneer (marinated in yogurt and spices, then grilled)
- 1/4 cup thinly sliced red onions
- 1/4 cup diced bell peppers
- Fresh cilantro for garnish

Instructions:

1. Preheat oven to 425°F (220°C).
2. Spread tikka masala sauce over the crust.
3. Add paneer, onions, and bell peppers.
4. Bake for 10-12 minutes.
5. Garnish with fresh cilantro before serving.

Malaysian Satay Pizza

Ingredients:

- 1 pizza crust
- 1/4 cup peanut satay sauce
- 1 cup grilled chicken strips marinated in satay spices
- 1/4 cup thinly sliced red onions
- 1/4 cup shredded mozzarella cheese
- Crushed peanuts and fresh cilantro for garnish

Instructions:

1. Preheat oven to 425°F (220°C).
2. Spread peanut satay sauce over the crust.
3. Add chicken, onions, and mozzarella.
4. Bake for 10-12 minutes.
5. Garnish with crushed peanuts and cilantro before serving.

Jamaican Ackee and Saltfish Pizza

Ingredients:

- 1 pizza crust
- 1/4 cup olive oil and garlic base
- 1/2 cup prepared ackee and saltfish (cooked with onions, peppers, and tomatoes)
- 1/4 cup shredded mozzarella (optional)
- Fresh thyme leaves for garnish

Instructions:

1. Preheat oven to 400°F (200°C).
2. Spread olive oil and garlic base over the crust.
3. Add ackee and saltfish mixture evenly.
4. Bake for 8-10 minutes until heated through.
5. Garnish with thyme before serving.

Thai Green Curry Pizza

Ingredients:

- 1 pizza crust
- 1/4 cup Thai green curry sauce
- 1/2 cup cooked chicken or shrimp
- 1/4 cup diced bell peppers
- 1/4 cup shredded mozzarella cheese
- Fresh Thai basil leaves for garnish

Instructions:

1. Preheat oven to 425°F (220°C).
2. Spread green curry sauce over the crust.
3. Add chicken/shrimp, peppers, and mozzarella.
4. Bake for 10-12 minutes.
5. Garnish with Thai basil before serving.

Moroccan Harissa Chicken Pizza

Ingredients:

- 1 pizza crust
- 1/4 cup harissa paste mixed with olive oil
- 1 cup grilled chicken strips marinated in Moroccan spices
- 1/4 cup sliced red onions
- 1/4 cup crumbled feta cheese
- Fresh mint leaves for garnish

Instructions:

1. Preheat oven to 425°F (220°C).
2. Spread harissa paste over the crust.
3. Add chicken, onions, and feta.
4. Bake for 10-12 minutes.
5. Garnish with fresh mint before serving.

Brazilian BBQ (Churrasco) Pizza

Ingredients:

- 1 pizza crust
- 1/4 cup Brazilian-style BBQ sauce
- 1 cup mixed grilled meats (beef, chicken, and sausage)
- 1/4 cup caramelized onions
- 1/4 cup shredded mozzarella cheese
- Chopped parsley for garnish

Instructions:

1. Preheat oven to 400°F (200°C).
2. Spread BBQ sauce over the crust.
3. Add grilled meats, onions, and mozzarella.
4. Bake for 10-12 minutes.
5. Garnish with parsley before serving.

Swiss Fondue Cheese Pizza

Ingredients:

- 1 pizza crust
- 1/2 cup fondue cheese mixture (Gruyère and Emmental melted with white wine)
- 1/4 cup diced potatoes (pre-cooked)
- 1/4 cup crispy bacon bits
- Freshly cracked black pepper

Instructions:

1. Preheat oven to 400°F (200°C).
2. Spread fondue cheese over the crust.
3. Add potatoes and bacon bits.
4. Bake for 8-10 minutes.
5. Sprinkle with black pepper before serving.

Hungarian Goulash Pizza

Ingredients:

- 1 pizza crust
- 1/4 cup paprika-infused tomato sauce
- 1 cup cooked goulash beef cubes
- 1/4 cup sautéed onions and peppers
- 1/4 cup shredded mozzarella cheese
- Fresh parsley for garnish

Instructions:

1. Preheat oven to 425°F (220°C).
2. Spread paprika tomato sauce over the crust.
3. Add goulash beef, onions, peppers, and mozzarella.
4. Bake for 10-12 minutes.
5. Garnish with parsley before serving.

Egyptian Fava Bean (Ful Medames) Pizza

Ingredients:

- 1 pizza crust
- 1/4 cup olive oil and lemon base
- 1/2 cup mashed fava beans (seasoned with cumin, garlic, and lemon)
- 1/4 cup diced tomatoes
- 1/4 cup chopped fresh parsley
- Crumbled feta cheese for garnish

Instructions:

1. Preheat oven to 400°F (200°C).
2. Spread olive oil and lemon mixture over the crust.
3. Add mashed fava beans, tomatoes, and parsley.
4. Bake for 8-10 minutes.
5. Garnish with feta cheese before serving.

Pakistani Seekh Kebab Pizza

Ingredients:

- 1 pizza crust
- 1/4 cup spiced tomato sauce
- 1 cup sliced seekh kebabs
- 1/4 cup red onion slices
- 1/4 cup shredded mozzarella cheese
- Fresh cilantro for garnish

Instructions:

1. Preheat oven to 425°F (220°C).
2. Spread spiced tomato sauce over the crust.
3. Add seekh kebab slices, onions, and mozzarella.
4. Bake for 10-12 minutes.
5. Garnish with cilantro before serving.

Indonesian Rendang Beef Pizza

Ingredients:

- 1 pizza crust
- 1/4 cup rendang curry sauce
- 1 cup shredded rendang beef
- 1/4 cup thinly sliced red chilies
- 1/4 cup shredded mozzarella cheese
- Fresh lime wedges for serving

Instructions:

1. Preheat oven to 400°F (200°C).
2. Spread rendang sauce over the crust.
3. Top with shredded beef, chilies, and mozzarella.
4. Bake for 10-12 minutes.
5. Serve with lime wedges.

French Croque Monsieur Pizza

Ingredients:

- 1 pizza crust
- 1/4 cup béchamel sauce
- 1/2 cup shredded Gruyère cheese
- 1/2 cup diced ham
- 1/4 cup grated Parmesan cheese

Instructions:

1. Preheat oven to 425°F (220°C).
2. Spread béchamel sauce over the crust.
3. Add ham, Gruyère, and Parmesan.
4. Bake for 10-12 minutes until golden and bubbly.

Chinese Peking Duck Pizza

Ingredients:

- 1 pizza crust
- 1/4 cup hoisin sauce
- 1 cup shredded Peking duck
- 1/4 cup thinly sliced green onions
- 1/4 cup shredded mozzarella cheese
- Cucumber slices for garnish

Instructions:

1. Preheat oven to 425°F (220°C).
2. Spread hoisin sauce over the crust.
3. Add duck, green onions, and mozzarella.
4. Bake for 10-12 minutes.
5. Garnish with cucumber slices before serving.

Italian Prosciutto and Fig Pizza

Ingredients:

- 1 pizza crust
- 1/4 cup fig jam
- 1/2 cup shredded mozzarella cheese
- 1/4 cup thinly sliced prosciutto
- Fresh arugula for garnish

Instructions:

1. Preheat oven to 400°F (200°C).
2. Spread fig jam over the crust.
3. Add mozzarella and prosciutto slices.
4. Bake for 8-10 minutes.
5. Top with arugula before serving.

Puerto Rican Mofongo Pizza

Ingredients:

- 1 pizza crust
- 1/4 cup garlic and olive oil sauce
- 1 cup mashed plantains (prepared as mofongo)
- 1/2 cup cooked pork chunks
- 1/4 cup shredded mozzarella cheese

Instructions:

1. Preheat oven to 425°F (220°C).
2. Spread garlic sauce over the crust.
3. Add mashed plantains, pork chunks, and mozzarella.
4. Bake for 10-12 minutes.

Scandinavian Smoked Salmon Pizza

Ingredients:

- 1 pizza crust
- 1/4 cup cream cheese
- 1/4 cup thinly sliced smoked salmon
- 1/4 cup capers
- Fresh dill for garnish

Instructions:

1. Preheat oven to 400°F (200°C).
2. Spread cream cheese over the crust.
3. Add smoked salmon and capers.
4. Bake for 8-10 minutes.
5. Garnish with fresh dill before serving.

Indian Samosa-Inspired Pizza

Ingredients:

- 1 pizza crust
- 1/4 cup spiced potato curry
- 1/4 cup green peas
- 1/4 cup shredded mozzarella cheese
- Tamarind chutney and fresh cilantro for garnish

Instructions:

1. Preheat oven to 425°F (220°C).
2. Spread spiced potato curry over the crust.
3. Add green peas and mozzarella.
4. Bake for 10-12 minutes.
5. Drizzle tamarind chutney and garnish with cilantro before serving.